SO YOU WANT TO BE AN INVENTOR?

SO
YOU WANT
TO BE
AN
INVENTOR?

BY

JUDITH
ST. GEORGE

ILLUSTRATED BY

DAVID
SMALL

SCHOLASTIC INC.

New York Toronto London Auckland Sydney
Mexico City New Delhi Hong Kong Buenos Aires

Are you a kid who likes to tinker with machines that clink and clank, levers that pull, bells that ring, cogs that grind, switches that turn on and off, wires that vibrate, dials that spin? You watch TV, ride a bike, phone your friends, pop popcorn in a microwave, go to the movies. Inventions! And you want to be an inventor, too?

You don't have to have white hair and wrinkles to be an inventor. At twelve, Benjamin Franklin invented swim paddles for his hands and kick paddles for his feet. When he grew up, Ben Franklin invented the lightning rod, Franklin stove, fireplace damper, library stepstool and odometer to measure the distance that a vehicle travels. At seventy-seven, he invented bifocal glasses. (He probably needed them!)

Do you have a brother? Brothers can help!

Connecticut patriot David Bushnell would have been sunk without his brother, Ezra. David wasn't strong enough to operate all the cranks, handles and pumps in the submarine he invented during the Revolutionary War, so Ezra did it for him.

In 1895, Guglielmo Marconi had his brother Alfonzo take a mile-and-a-half hike with a receiver and a gun. If he received the signals Guglielmo sent, he was to fire the gun. POW! That gunshot broadcast the birth of Guglielmo's invention—the radio!

If you want to be an inventor, find a need and fill it.

Cyrus McCormick got tired of reaping wheat on his family's farm with a hand scythe. It took forever! So in 1831, he invented a mechanical reaper. The flapping reaper frightened the horses. BUT it reaped in a few hours what three men could reap in a day.

The son of runaway slaves, Elijah McCoy was an oilman on a railroad. To oil the pistons, gears and bearings, the train had to be stopped. In 1872, he invented a lubricator that oiled the pistons, gears and bearings while the engine was running! Other workers wanted his invention for their engines. But they wanted "the real McCoy" lubricators—or nothing!

If you want to be an inventor, be a dreamer.

As a boy in Scotland, Alexander Graham Bell had a "dreaming place." When he grew up, he dreamed of people talking across distances—maybe by electric signals. Electric signals it was! In 1876, he invented the telephone!

Young Russian Igor Sikorsky dreamed of a different way to fly—up, down, forward, backward, AND sideways. Igor's brother poked fun at him. "It will never fly!" He was wrong. With its three blades whirling, in 1939 Igor's dream helicopter took off.

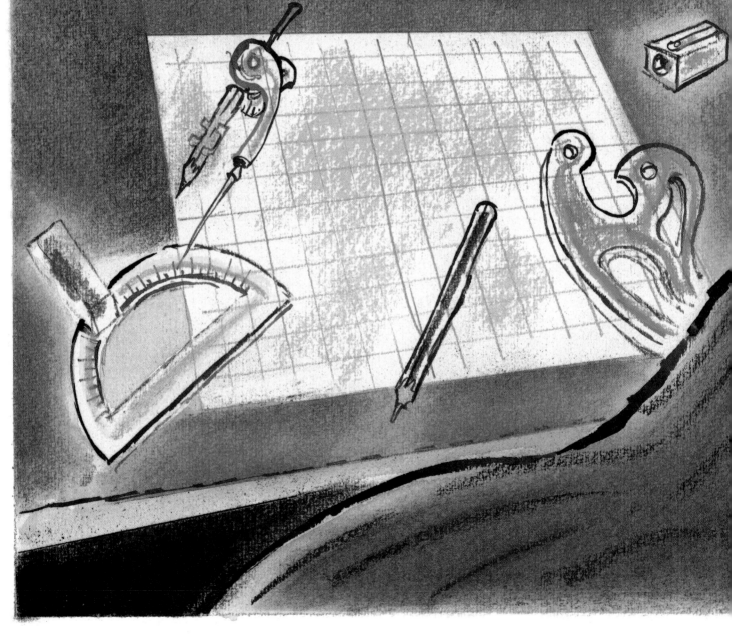

If you want to be an inventor, keep your eyes open!

On a 1914 trip to Labrador, fur trader Clarence Birdseye watched Eskimos freeze fish on the ice. When the fish thawed, they tasted fresh. Would fast-freezing food between two metal plates work as well? It did! All those frozen dinners, pizzas and other frozen yummies come to you by way of Clarence Birdseye.

After a country walk with his dog in 1948, Swiss engineer Georges de Mestral picked cockleburs off his pants. Why, the cocklebur hooks gripped the wool loops in his pants. Hooks and loops! The perfect fastener! Georges's invention? Velcro!

An inventor has to be as stubborn as a bulldog.

Yankee Charles Goodyear spent ten years trying to make raw rubber usable. He spent all his money and was thrown into debtor's jail before he hit the jackpot in 1839 by treating raw rubber with sulphur under heat. Tires, tennis balls, and all sorts of other rubber goodies have been bouncing around ever since!

Thomas Edison spent more than a year looking for a thin thread called a filament that would glow without burning up when electricity passed through it. He tried platinum, nickel, gold, silver, fish line, cotton thread, coconut hair, people hair, wood shavings, cork and more. Carbonized bamboo was the answer! Edison's 1879 incandescent lamp (a lamp that stayed lit) brightened lives everywhere.

Don't worry if people laugh at you.

Everyone mocked Robert Fulton's steamboat, calling it "Fulton's Folly" and "a floating sawmill caught on fire." But the laughter lost steam in 1807 when Robert's *Clermont* chugged up the Hudson River from New York to Albany with paddle wheels churning and flags waving.

Newspapers laughed at Robert Goddard for trying to invent a space rocket. They called him "Moon Man." And a hoaxer. He was no hoaxer! Thanks to "Moon Man" Robert Goddard's 1926 invention of a liquid-fuel rocket, the spacecraft *Apollo 11* landed Americans safely on the moon in 1969.

Inventors aren't all men!

Illinois homemaker Josephine Cochran figured other women were as fed up with washing dishes (and red hands) as she was. In 1886, she put together a wooden tub, wire basket and hand pump to invent the very first dishwasher.

Movie star Hedy Lamarr said, "Any girl can look glamorous. All you have to do is stand still and look stupid." Beautiful Hedy Lamarr wasn't stupid! Just before World War II she fled Austria (and Hitler) for the United States, where she and a friend invented a system for guiding torpedoes by radio signals. Her goal? Beat Hitler!

Even Presidents can be inventors.

George Washington invented a sixteen-sided treading barn in 1792. Horses trampled over wheat spread on the barn floor. The grain dropped through slots. Eureka! George Washington's wheat supply was dry, stored and ready to be ground into flour.

Thomas Jefferson invented a two-faced clock, one face inside (it told the day, hour, minute—and second) and one face outside (its Chinese gong could be heard three miles away). Jefferson wasn't called smart for nothing. The ropes holding the weights were so long that he cut holes in the floor to let the weights hang in the basement!

Maybe you like to work alone. Alexander Graham Bell worked alone at night, every night, inventing the graphaphone, an iron lung, kites to study flight and, of course, the telephone. "To take night from me is to rob me of life," he declared.

Nikola Tesla was world famous for inventing the alternating-current (AC) motor in the 1880s to produce huge amounts of electricity that could be sent over long distances. But Nikola lived in lonely New York hotel rooms, had no family, few friends, and only worked for himself.

Maybe you'd rather invent as part of a team.

Thomas Edison forged a crew of inventors who huddled day (and night) over clanking, hissing motors, smelly chemicals and machines that sent sparks flying. He—and his crew—came up with the incandescent lamp, the movie camera, the phonograph and more than a thousand other inventions!

One invention can lead to another.

In the early 1900s, Henry Ford jumped from Michigan Farmboy to King of the Road. He didn't invent the automobile, BUT he did perfect mass production and the moving assembly line that had workers slapping his Model T Ford cars together in a hurry.

Other inventors hopped on board. Mary Anderson invented windshield wipers. (Swish-swish!) Garrett Morgan came up with traffic lights. (Red—stop! Yellow—slow! Green—go!) Elmer Wavering invented car radios. (A little music, please!) More cars? More accidents? Allen Breed's air bags saved lives. (Whoosh!)

Wouldn't Henry Ford be amazed at what he had started!

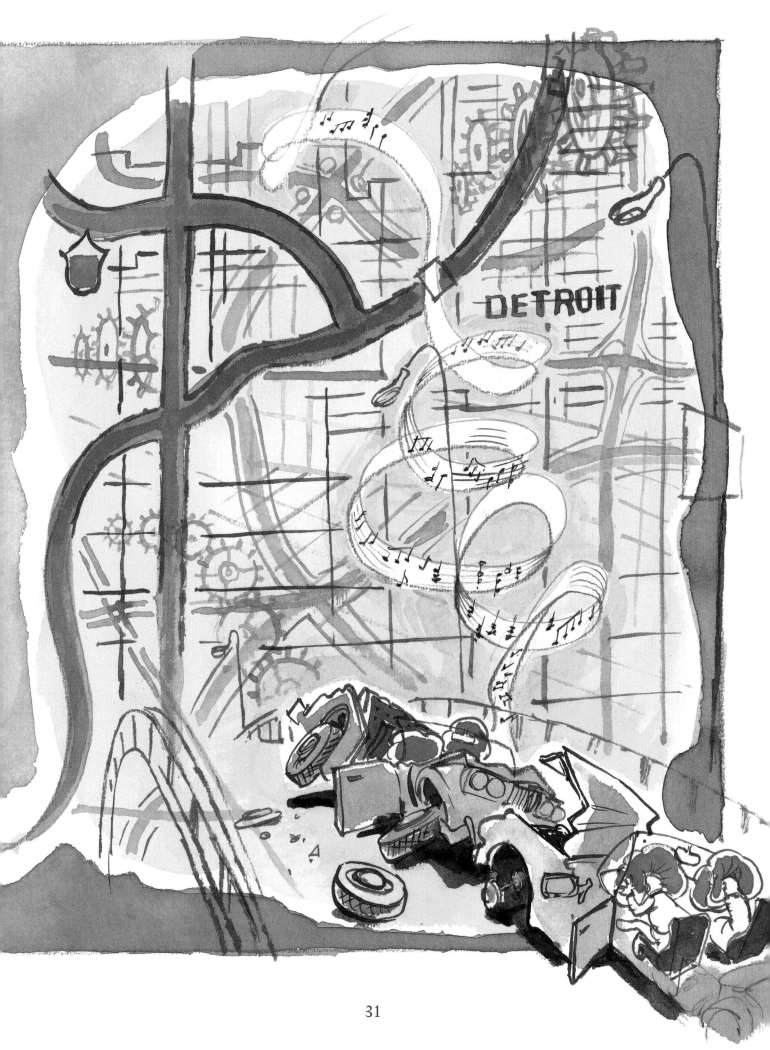

Sometimes an invention creates more problems than it solves.

In 1793, Eli Whitney invented the cotton gin that cleaned cotton fifty times faster than workers cleaning by hand. (Wire spikes pulled cotton through slots too narrow for the seeds.) But more and more slaves were needed to grow more and more cotton. Eli Whitney's cotton gin sowed the seeds of the Civil War!

Watch out! Your invention might scare people.

Swedish chemist Alfred Nobel invented dynamite in 1866 by mixing nitroglycerin with chalky soil. But when five workers were killed in an explosion, Alfred was ordered to work outside the city on a barge in the middle of a lake.

While experimenting in 1895, scientist Wilhelm Roentgen was shocked when he turned on an electric switch and saw light rays glowing from a screen he had treated with barium. X rays! People freaked out. Did seeing their own bones mean they would die? Or were X rays really death rays?

Be careful! The truth is, inventing can be dangerous.

At an 1854 New York City fair, Elisha Otis stood on a platform that was raised up thirty feet by rope. He ordered the rope cut. The platform fell! But iron teeth grabbed notches in the guide rails and stopped the platform cold. "All safe, gentlemen, all safe!" Elisha called out. His safety-brake invention worked!

Some of Orville and Wilbur Wright's early-1900s flying machines landed safely and some didn't. Poor Orville! He was hurt in a glider crash, two airplane crashes and a plane crash that knocked him out and broke his leg and ribs! "Flying machine, cloth, and sticks in a heap, with me in the center," Orville wrote in his diary.

Some inventions are invented before their time.

If Leonardo da Vinci hadn't been born more than five hundred and fifty years ago, he could have been one of the greatest! He thought up (and sketched) an air cooling machine, automobile, paddle wheel boat, diver's snorkel, flying machine, parachute and projector for pictures.

In the 1830s, British mathematician Charles Babbage invented a steam-powered "computer" that had a memory bank, made decisions and recorded data. His idea was on target, but his computer had to be trashed for lack of electronic know-how.

Keep a sharp eye on your invention—copycats are out there!

Joseph Henry invented a telegraph system in the 1830s that sent signals over short distances. In 1844, Samuel F. B. Morse jazzed up Joseph's invention, put together a Morse code dot-dash system, and was tapped as inventor of the telegraph.

In 1847, William Kelly invented a method of producing steel by burning off excess carbon in hot pig iron with a blast of cold air. Eight years later, Henry Bessemer's mammoth, flame-shooting converters produced steel the same way. Who was known as the red-hot steel maker? Henry Bessemer, that's who!

Of course, some inventions never take off at all.

Andrew Jackson Jr. invented adjustable eyeglasses for chickens so that they wouldn't peck each other's eyes out. (The chickens weren't interested!)

John Boax invented a haircutting helmet that sucked hair up into tiny holes where electric coils burned hair to just the right length. (Ouch!)

Elmer Walter invented a table knife with a mirror on the handle to use at meals for checking if food was stuck in his teeth. (Disgusting!)

Franz Vester invented a coffin with an escape hatch and a breathing tube in case the person inside was still alive. (Too gruesome!)

Other inventions take off so well, they're named for their inventor.

Electricity is measured in volts (Alessandro Volta invented the electric battery) and watts (James Watt made steam power practical).

Charles Macintosh's weatherproof fabric turned into mackintosh raincoats.

During the French Revolution, Joseph Guillotin's guillotine beheaded victims.

Rudolf Diesel invented the diesel engine that runs on unrefined oil.

Here's the bottom line! Whether your invention is named after you or not, whether you're a dreamer, a loner, are laughed at, work all night or put yourself in danger, your invention could change the world. It has happened!

Vladimir Zworykin's 1923 electronic tube led to television.

Three U.S. scientists' 1947 transistor led to computers.

Even more important, Johannes Gutenberg invented a hand-operated printing press with movable metal type in the 1440s. A printer could print in a day what it took a year to write by hand. Result? Books! Books! Books! People decided it was time to learn to read. And they did!

In the end, being an inventor means pushing the limits of what human beings know and what human beings can do. Because you're a risk taker and will be on a quest into the unknown, you have to be willing to try and fail, try and fail, try and MAYBE succeed.

One thing is certain: There will always be barriers to be broken, whether it's to find a new source of power, a different way to communicate, a machine that works medical miracles or something that we can't even imagine. It takes passion and heart, but those barriers could be broken by you!

BIOGRAPHICAL NOTES

Babbage, Charles (1792–1871)—British mathematics professor Babbage also invented a speedometer and an ophthalmoscope that examines the inner eye.

Bell, Alexander Graham (1847–1922)—Although famous for his inventions, Scottish-born Bell always described himself as a teacher of speech to the deaf.

Bessemer, Sir Henry (1813–1898)—British engineer Bessemer's process for mass-producing steel made low-cost steel available for construction and industry.

Birdseye, Clarence (1886–1956)—In 1949, Brooklyn native Birdseye invented a dehydration process that preserved food by removing all the water.

Bushnell, David (1742–1824)—Yale graduate Bushnell was first to make a time bomb and first to prove that gunpowder could be exploded underwater.

Cochran, Josephine (1841–1913)—Cochran set up a company to manufacture dishwashers for hotels and restaurants—homeowners found them too pricey!

de Mestral, Georges (1907–1990)—De Mestral had an instant idea, but designing tools and machinery to produce Velcro's stiff hooks and soft loops took eight years.

Diesel, Rudolf (1858–1913)—Both transportation and industry benefited from German engineer Diesel's 1897 invention of the internal combustion engine.

Edison, Thomas (1847–1931)—Of Ohio native Edison's 1,093 inventions, his greatest was his invention factory that turned out nothing but inventions.

Ford, Henry (1863–1947)—Michigan farmer's son Ford was the first to produce a simple, cheap, reliable car that the average American could afford.

Franklin, Benjamin (1706–1790)—A writer, publisher, statesman, scientist and inventor, Boston-born Franklin was famous for his experiments with electricity.

Fulton, Robert (1765–1815)—A popular artist who studied engineering, Pennsylvanian Fulton also designed and successfully tested a submarine.

Goddard, Robert (1882–1945)—Massachusetts professor Goddard's inventions led to the development of modern rocketry, satellites and space travel.

Goodyear, Charles (1800–1860)—Although Connecticut native Goodyear had no scientific training, he gained lasting fame by vulcanizing rubber.

Guillotin, Joseph (1738–1814)—French medical doctor Guillotin believed that his guillotine invention executed a condemned person mercifully and painlessly.

Gutenberg, Johannes (1397?–1468)—Born in Mainz, Germany, Gutenberg printed his masterpiece, a two-volume Bible known as the Gutenberg Bible, in the 1450s.

Henry, Joseph (1797–1878)—New York physicist Henry's extensive knowledge of electricity and magnetism led to the first practical electric motor.

Jefferson, Thomas (1743–1826)—Virginian Jefferson also invented a wooden plow, a swivel chair and a wheel cipher that coded and decoded messages.

Kelly, William (1811–1888)—Pittsburgh ironmaster Kelly invented a converter to produce steel that was a major improvement over wrought iron.

Lamarr, Hedy (1914–2000)—Glamorous Lamarr and her companion, George Antheil, invented a system that became the basis for satellite communication.

Leonardo da Vinci (1452–1519)—Italian Leonardo was an artist, architect, scientist, inventor, engineer and musician—one of history's great geniuses.

Macintosh, Charles (1766–1843)—In 1823, Scottish chemist Macintosh invented waterproof fabric by bonding two fabrics together with a liquid rubber cement.

Marconi, Guglielmo (1874–1937)—Italian-born physicist Marconi, who invented a wireless telegraph system, also designed a transatlantic wireless signal.

McCormick, Cyrus (1809-1884)—Farming was changed forever when Virginian McCormick's mechanical reaper made cultivation of vast areas of land possible.

McCoy, Elijah (1844-1929)—After African-Canadian McCoy was educated as a master mechanic and engineer in Scotland, he worked on a Michigan railroad.

Morse, Samuel F. B. (1791-1872)—A portrait painter and inventor, Yale graduate Morse developed a telegraph system that sent messages over long distances.

Nobel, Alfred (1833-1896)—Unhappy that his dynamite was used for destruction and war, Swedish chemist Nobel established the Nobel Prize for Peace in his will.

Otis, Elisha (1811-1861)—The son of a Vermont farmer, Otis also designed a steam-powered elevator, railroad cars and brakes, a steam plow and a bake oven.

Roentgen, Wilhelm (1845-1923)—German physics professor Roentgen's discovery of X rays revolutionized medical diagnosis, therapy and techniques.

Sikorsky, Igor (1889-1972)—In addition to his helicopter, Russian-born American Sikorsky designed both four-engined aircraft and amphibious aircraft.

Tesla, Nikola (1856-1943)—After arriving in this country in 1884, Croatian-born electrical engineer Tesla perfected his alternating-current induction motor.

Three U.S. scientists—**John Bardeen** (1908-1991), **Walter Brattain** (1902-1987), and **William Shockley** (1910-1989)—won the 1956 Nobel Prize for their transistor.

Volta, Alessandro (1745-1827)—Italian physicist Volta invented the forerunner of the electric condenser and the electrophorus, a device for storing electric charge.

Washington, George (1732-1799)—Washington used fish waste for fertilizer, rotated crops and worked to prevent soil erosion on his Virginia plantation.

Watt, James (1736-1819)—Watt, who was a Scottish shopkeeper's son, helped to usher in the Industrial Revolution with his improved steam engine design.

Whitney, Eli (1765-1825)—New Englander Whitney also owned a factory that manufactured muskets using interchangeable parts on an assembly line—a first.

Wright, Orville (1871-1948), **Wilbur** (1867-1912)—Raised in Ohio, the Wright brothers flew kites and gliders before experimenting with motorized airplanes.

Zworykin, Vladimir (1889-1982)—Russian-American Zworykin also invented the electron microscope, which made viruses and protein molecules visible.

BIBLIOGRAPHY

Aaseng, Nathan. **The Inventors: Nobel Prizes in Chemistry, Physics, and Medicine.** Minneapolis: Lerner Publications, 1988.

Blow, Michael. **Men of Science and Invention.** New York: American Heritage Publishing, 1960.

Breeden, Robert L., Ed. **Those Inventive Americans.** Washington, D.C.: National Geographic Society, 1971.

Cooke, David C. **Inventions That Made History.** New York: G. P. Putnam's Sons, 1968.

Feldman, Anthony, and Peter Ford. **Scientists & Inventors.** New York: Facts on File, 1979.

Jeffries, Michael, and Gary A. Lewis. **Inventors and Inventions.** New York: Smithmark Publishers, 1992.

Manchester, Harland. **Trail Blazers of Technology.** New York: Charles Scribner's Sons, 1962.

Murphy, Jim. **Weird & Wacky Inventions.** New York: Crown Publishers, 1978.

Platt, Richard. **Smithsonian Visual Timeline of Inventions.** New York: Dorling Kindersley Publishing, 1994.

Smith, Richard M., Ed. **Newsweek Extra: The Power of Invention.** New York: Newsweek, Winter 1997-1998.

Love to James and his family
—J.St.G.

To Sarah
—D.S.

Patrica Lee Gauch, editor

ISBN 0-439-57589-3

12 11 10 9 8 7 6 5 4 3 2 1   3 4 5 6 7 8/0

Printed in the U.S.A.   40

First Scholastic printing, October 2003

Book design by Semadar Megged

The text is set in Golden Type ITC.
The art was done in ink, watercolor, and pastel chalk.

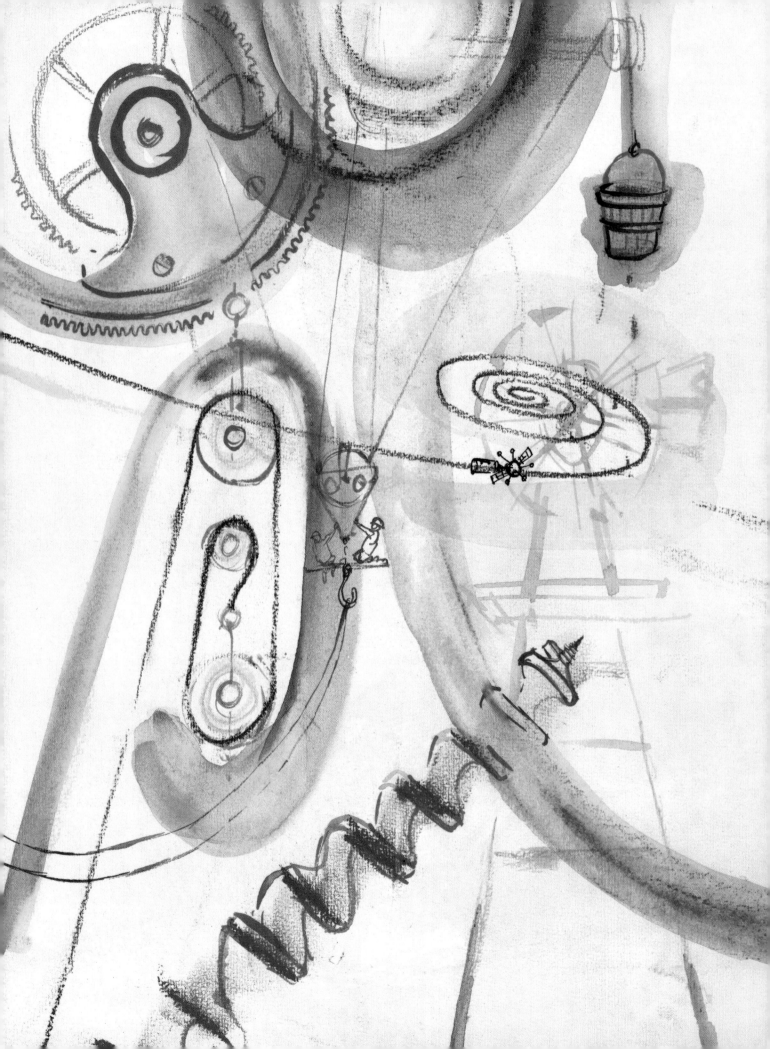